99½
Creepy Crawly Jokes, Riddles, & Nonsense

Written and illustrated
by Holly Kowitt

SCHOLASTIC INC.
New York   Toronto   London   Auckland   Sidney

ISBN 0-590-93993-9

Copyright © 1997 by Holly Kowitt.
All rights reserved. Published by Scholastic Inc.

12 11 10 9 8 7 6 5 4 3 2   7 8 9/9 0 1 2/0

Printed in the U.S.A.   40
First Scholastic printing, April 1997

For John Carini

Special thanks to Kate Egan

WHAT'S THE BUZZ?

What did the chair say to the termite?

"You bore me!"

What did one firefly say to another?

"You glow, girl!"

What did one snake say to another?

"Let's see you worm your way out of this one!"

What did one bee say to another?

"Mind your own buzzness!"

What did one worm say to another?

"Where on earth have you been?"

YOU BUG ME

What do you call a fly who likes to sing but doesn't know the words?

A humbug.

What does a mosquito use to keep her hair in place?

Bug spray.

How do bugs find out the news?

They read the flypaper.

Why did the mosquito go to the Old Bugs Home?

To visit a great-ant.

Why did the moth eat the firefly?

He wanted a light snack.

FLEA-FOR-ALL

What do you get when a bug opens a motel?

A real fleabag.

How can you tell if a flea belongs to you?

Just look at his flea collar.

Daddy Flea: How are the kids?
Mommy Flea: Going to the dogs!

FANGS BUT NO FANGS!

Did you hear about the boy who swallows cassettes?

He got tapeworm!

What's a snake's favorite veggie?

Asp-aragus.

How did the earthworm afford a new home?

He got it dirt cheap.

What do snakes do after they fight?

Hiss and make up.

What does a boa constrictor call his dinner date?

Dessert.

Why do snakes collect baseball cards?

Because boas will be boas.

What do you call a snake in a demolition derby?

A crashing boa.

HOW DO YOU TELL A CREEPY CRAWLY TO GET LOST?

Fly: Bug off!

Leech: Get off my back!

Lice: Get out of my hair!

Firefly: Glow away!

Wood tick: Take a hike!

16

QUESTIONS AND ANT-SWERS

What does an ant take for an upset stomach?
Ant-acid.

What's that metal rod on top of an anthill?
An ant-enna.

What do you call an old ant?

An ant-ique.

Where do ants go on vacation?

Ant-arctica.

What do ants like on their pizza?

Ant-chovies.

What's an ant's favorite animal?

An ant-elope.

What part of a moose does an ant like best?

His ant-lers.

CREEPY CRAWLIES IN SCHOOL

Are snakes good at math?

Just the adders.

What's a python's favorite subject?

Hiss-tory.

Where does a butterfly learn long division?

From his moth teacher.

Why did the wasp get sent to the principal's office?

He misbee-hived.

Why didn't the inchworm make the honor roll?

He didn't measure up.

What class activity do fireflies enjoy the most?

Glow-and-tell.

How did the earthworm do in school?

He's at the bottom of his class.

Why did the termite leave school with a chair?

The teacher told him to take a seat.

Why do fireflies do well in school?

They're very bright!

Where do insects go when they
talk back to the teacher?

To see the lice principal.

SNAKES IN SCHOOL
...to the flag, of the UNITED SNAKES of AMERICA...

KNOCK-KNOCKS THAT WILL DRIVE YOU BUGGY

Knock-knock.
Who's there?
Spider.
Spider who?
Spider in the kitchen, eating bugs again!

Knock-knock.
Who's there?
Bug spray.
Bug spray who?
Bugs pray that snakes won't eat them!

Knock-knock.
Who's there?
Katydid.
Katydid who?
Katy didn't want to hear any more knock-knock jokes!

Knock-knock.
Who's there?
Anthill.
Anthill who?
Aunt Hilda's eating bugs again!

Knock-knock.
Who's there?
Ladybug.
Ladybug who?
Lady, bug somebody else for a change!

BEE A SPORT

What do you get when bugs play baseball?

Fly balls.

Did you hear about the silkworms who ran a relay race?

They ended up in a tie.

FIREFLY PARENTS

Why don't cobras like baseball?

Because they get only three strikes.

What do you get from a flea who plays basketball?

Cootie shots.

How does a firefly start a relay race?

"Ready, set, glow!"

How do snakes swim across a river?

They do the crawl.

Why do spiders make good outfielders?

They catch a lot of flies.

BUGS AND KISSES

What do you call a fifty-pound hornet with a slime gun?

Sir.

How is the Blob like a can of bug spray?

They both repel insects!

Do bugs go to the mall?

No, just the flea market.

What is a caterpillar?

A worm in a fuzzy sweater.

What do mosquitos complain about when they're on vacation?

"Too many people!"

Why did the termite put on pajamas?

He was going to a lumber party.

What do you say to a firefly who runs into a window?

"Way to glow!"

BUG OFF!

What do you call a spider who's had too much sugar?

A jitterbug.

What kind of fly gets asked to leave the park?

A litterbug.

What kind of insect has the best manners?

A ladybug.

If the Blob were an insect, what would he be?

A stinkbug.

CREEPY CRAWLIES
AND COMPUTERS

What do mosquitos fear most about computers?

The Net.

How do bugs send computer messages?

By flea-mail.

Did you hear about the spider that lives in a computer?

He has his own web site.

Why do termites like computers?

They get to log on!

SNAKES ALIVE!

How does an earthworm turn down a party invitation?

"Thanks, but I'm not in the mud."

What do you call a King Cobra?

Hiss Majesty.

What toy does a baby snake like best?

His rattle.

What does a python say when you give him a nice, juicy rat?

"Fangs a lot!"

Why are snakes easy to weigh?

They have lots of scales.

What happens to earthworms who misbehave?

They get grounded.

Why did the snake go to the doctor?

He was feeling low.

What does a python call a guinea pig?

An appetizer.

Where do worms go on vacation?

The Big Apple.

JUST PULLING YOUR LEGS!

Why did the spider become a DJ?

So he could spin records.

What do you call a spider who's eaten too many flies?

Fatty long-legs.

Where can you see tarantulas dance?

At a hairball.

What do you call a spider who makes salad?

A salad spinner!

What do you call spiders who just got married?

Newlywebs.

HAVE YOU EVER SEEN...?

...a fly fishing?

...a mosquito bite?

...a house fly?

...a moth ball?

...a honey comb?

...a snakeskin?

FAMILY REUNION

DON'T WORRY, BEE HAPPY

How do you congratulate a bumblebee?
Give him a high hive.

What do you call a bee who never brags?
A humble-bee.

What do beekeepers need when they study?

Some bees and quiet.

What kind of bath does a bee take?

A bumble bath.

What kind of gum do bees chew?

Bumble gum.

Why did the bee join a rock band?

To be the lead stinger.

WHAT'S YOUR PET COBRA KNOWN FOR?

What's your pet cobra known for?

His striking looks.

What's your pet mosquito known for?

His biting wit.

What's your pet bee known for?

His stinging remarks.

What's your pet termite known for?

His boring personality.

What's your firefly known for?

His bright ideas.

DID YOU HEAR THE ONE ABOUT...?

Did you hear the one about the giant hornet?

Never mind, it's over your head.

Did you hear the one about the maggot pudding?

Never mind, you'd never swallow it.

Did you hear the one about the bedbug who went on strike?

It's just a mite revolting.

Did you hear the one about the electric eel?

It's a shocker!

SLUGS AND KISSES

What do salamanders watch every night at six?

The evening newts.

Why is it hard to fool a slug?

'Cause you can't pull his leg!

How do you stop the Blob from eating worms?

Give him a good slug.

What's a lizard's favorite phone service?

Call wading.

HALF JOKE

Knock-knock.
Who's there?
Amos.
Amos who?
A mosquito just bit me on the _____!